Why Worship
Matters

Robert A. Rimbo

Augsburg Fortress

WHY WORSHIP MATTERS

Unless otherwise indicated, Scripture quotations are from the New Revised Standard Version Bible © 1989 Division of Christian Education of the National Council of the Churches of Christ in the United States of America. Used by permission.

Editors: Suzanne Burke, Robert Farlee, Jessica Hillstrom
Cover and interior design: Laurie Ingram
Cover photo © Nathan Benn/CORBIS

ISBN 0-8066-5108-3

Manufactured in the U.S.A.

07   06   05   04   1   2   3   4   5   6   7   8   9   10

Contents

Foreword

In our often frenetic lives too seldom do we take time for thoughtful reflection and engaging conversation about things that are important. Bishop Robert Rimbo makes a clear and compelling case why he thinks worship matters and why worship deserves—even requires—our thoughtful attention and engaging conversation.

Worship is central to the Christian life. The crucified and risen Christ is present at the center of the assembly gathered around the means of grace. Through the word proclaimed and sacraments celebrated, the Holy Spirit is at work. Lives are changed. Sins are forgiven. The alienated are reconciled. Strangers are welcomed. Unbelief gives way to faith. God is praised. Worship matters!

Bishop Rimbo persuasively reminds us that worship is not a means to some other end. The Christ present for us in worship meets us in the world. Worship connects us to God's mission for the life of the world. Christ present in word and sacrament joins us to suffering humanity and the fragile creation. Worship matters!

Bishop Rimbo writes out of his experience as a pastor and worship leader who, in congregational ministry and now serving local worshiping assemblies as synodical bishop, has remembered "that the church is a house filled with treasures old and new." He is committed to the proposition that, "as God's people beyond the limit of space and time, we are linked to all God's people in the past and to all those yet to come. We need both continuity with our heritage and constant reformation."

Some may take issue with Bishop Rimbo's views of "contemporary" styles of worship. Others may challenge his theological assumptions. Yet all should agree that worship matters! This helpful book is an invitation for you to join an important and rich conversation that pushes beyond issues of how we worship to why we worship.

Mark S. Hanson
Presiding Bishop
Evangelical Lutheran Church in America

Preface

This little book is a kind of conversation. As such it contains hard sayings and sweet sentiments. It's not scholarly but it grows out of serious liturgical study, most of which has been within congregations rather than classrooms. It invites you to think and talk.

Although the opinions are mine, I am deeply indebted to many people who have helped shape me as a participant in the assembly gathered around word and sacraments. Despite the great danger in making lists, I must share some of their names: Arthur Carl Piepkorn, Joel Kuznik, Herbert Lindemann, George W. Hoyer, John Tietjen, and John Damm (all professors); Eugene L. Brand (my mentor, friend, and boss as we worked together on *Lutheran Book of Worship*); the people of God at Lutheran churches where I have been privileged to serve: Mount Olive (Minneapolis, Minnesota), Grace (Teaneck, New Jersey), St. Paul (Valley Stream, New York), St. James (Grosse Pointe, Michigan), Antioch (Farmington Hills, Michigan), and the various congregations of the Southeast Michigan Synod of the Evangelical Lutheran Church in America.

As I read this manuscript (again and again) I find it increasingly difficult to distinguish my voice from the voices of others. I am especially aware of the influence of Gordon Lathrop and Marva Dawn who have been champions of faithful worship and have shaped my understanding in profound ways. I am indebted to them and many others.

I have likewise gained insight and wisdom from the Board of The Liturgical Conference, the Homiletics Seminar of the North American Academy of Liturgy, the Advisory Council of Valparaiso University's Institute of Liturgical Studies and my participation in the Association of Lutheran Church Musicians.

And finally, I am indebted to my spouse, Lois, and our children, Deborah and Justin (and our recent addition, Justin's spouse, Angela) all of whom have been faithful members of the assembly. Beyond that, Lois has been a patient practitioner of Christian formation (while her spouse was leading worship and she was tending to children and Cheerios), a compassionate critic of sermons in process and how we go about welcoming people into the presence of God, and an active participant in the life of the congregations to which she has belonged. To my family, I dedicate this little book, as well as to the larger family of God of which by grace we are members.

Robert Alan Rimbo
The Holy Trinity, 2004

1
Ends and Beginnings

Here is an opportunity I could not pass by: to write about *why worship matters.*

I have a friend who is a great fan of mystery novels. He has a peculiar habit of reading the last chapter first. I could never do that with a mystery novel, but I want to urge you to do that now.

As I begin, I remind myself and, more importantly, I remind you that what I say here is subjective, personal. But it's also (I hope) pastoral and communal. As I approach the thirtieth anniversary of my ordination and begin my second term as a bishop in the Evangelical Lutheran Church in America, I have hopes and dreams for worship not only in our "corner of the vineyard" (because of the promising work of Renewing Worship*)* but for the church catholic.

I invite you into a conversation in which I hope you will engage with others as well as with me. To start, I want to talk about the "ends" I have in my mind and spirit. All that follows on these pages are my hopes growing from the renewal that began with the Second Vatican Council and continued through the Inter-Lutheran Commission on Worship (and countless other places) and, now continuing in the remarkable work of the Evangelical Lutheran Church in America and its publishing house, Augsburg Fortress.

When I think about "ends" I am reminded of T. S. Eliot's *Four Quartets,* specifically my favorite poem, "Little Gidding." Little Gidding is a hamlet in Cambridgeshire, England, where a religious community was founded by Nicholas Ferrar in 1625. Ferrar was inspired both by the Catholic and Protestant teachings of his time and wanted to create a community where the best of both could be used in harmony, which is also appealing to me. And it worked, at least for a time. Although the community sought seclusion from the world, people were interested in the way of life they had established. In 1936, three hundred years after its founding, Thomas Stearns Eliot was captivated by the place and wrote a poem inspired by his visits. I quote only a small portion:

> What we call the beginning is often the end
> And to make an end is to make a beginning.
> The end is where we start from. . . .
> We shall not cease from exploration
> And the end of all our exploring
> Will be to arrive where we started
> And know the place for the first time.
> —T. S. Eliot, *Collected Poems 1909–1962*

The end of this renewal for which we long and work is not that I want a place for *me,* for my best creations in music and art, for my homiletical masterpieces to be on display, for my opinion and my tastes to reign supreme, for people like me to gather.

The end I am hoping for and working for is found in the resources for renewal which began for me and many others with the publication of *Lutheran Book of Worship* (1978) and the other worship resources in a trajectory of publication since then (from Lutheran publishers and others; in fact, I see traces of *Lutheran Book of Worship* in many newer worship books). We have by no means exhausted what *Lutheran*

Book of Worship and its supplements offer. So one of the ends for which I hope is that we will continually examine and critique our worship. In this sense, of course, the end is where we start from and

> the end of all our exploring
> Will be to arrive where we started
> And know the place for the first time.

But much more awaits us. And I want to write about that "more," too. So let me try to articulate my hopes for our ongoing life as the assembly gathered around word and sacrament, that remarkable group of people who faithfully say and do the gospel of Jesus Christ in worship. Our language includes many uses for the word *assembly*, including constitutional uses, but in this book I use it to mean the people gathered for worship. Let me share with you my ideas on why worship matters.

For reflection and discussion

1. Why does worship matter to you?
2. What are your hopes for worship in your congregation? Write them here as a reminder.

2
Worship Matters Because God Is Worth It

I don't know how many times I have said or written these words: "The grace of our Lord Jesus Christ, the love of God, and the communion of the Holy Spirit be with you all" (2 Cor. 13:13). They appear at the top of many letters and at the beginning of many services.

The heart of the church's ministry is leading people to God, to what this verse says. So the first truth about "why worship matters" is "God matters." We worship because God is worth worshiping.

Such a reason would seem to be obvious. But I wonder. And that wondering will be in, with, and under all the words I am writing. It's a wondering based on far-reaching experiences of worshiping with God's people around the world in such diverse places as the General Assembly of the Mbulu Diocese of the Evangelical Lutheran Church in Tanzania, the Church of the Redeemer in Jerusalem, and the Uppsala Cathedral of the Church of Sweden. In such places the central things of the *ordo* hold together even when I don't know the language being used. These wondering experiences are also based on countless services in congregations in southeast Michigan, in my home congregation and in various assemblies around the United

States. It's a wondering profoundly influenced by a concern that sometimes we are more interested in leading people to church membership and only secondarily with leading people to God. It's a wondering based on the fact that our mission is not only to "the great unwashed" but also to "the washed," not only to those "out there" but also to those "in here," not only to the world but to the church.

But this worship is, first, God-ward. The Right Reverend N. T. Wright, biblical scholar and Anglican bishop of Durham, expresses the centrality of God in our worship when he writes:

> How can you cope with the end of a world and the beginning of another one? How can you put an earthquake into a test-tube, or the sea into a bottle? How can you live with the terrifying thought that the hurricane has become human, that fire has become flesh, that life itself came to life and walked in our midst? Christianity either means that, or it means nothing. It is either the most devastating disclosure of the deepest reality in the world, or it's a sham, a nonsense, a bit of deceitful play-acting. Most of us, unable to cope with saying either of those things, condemn ourselves to live in the shallow world in between. We may not be content there, but we don't know how to escape. . . .
>
> [The] way through is by sheer unadulterated worship of the living and true God, and by following this God wherever he leads, whether or not it is the way our traditions would suggest. Worship is not an optional extra for the Christian, a self-indulgent religious activity. It is the basic Christian stance, and indeed (so Christians claim) the truly human stance. "Worship" derives from "worth-ship": it means giving God all he's worth (Wright, p. 1).

These few words from Bishop Wright capture the essence of his entire book, *For All God's Worth,* which I recommend to you. I believe that who Jesus is and what he does are most reliably encountered in word and sacraments: in the scriptures proclaimed, in the washing with water in the name of the triune God, and in the meal of Jesus's own self-giving. These concrete, real things connect us to God and to the church. They welcome us to the full truth about ourselves and our world: sin and forgiveness, sorrow and hope, hunger and food, loneliness and community, death and life are all met here. Indeed, as Dr. Wright cleverly writes later in this same volume:

> It is right, therefore, that from time to time the church should take stock of that which is most central, most important, most vital in our common life together. Though we sing with the tongues of [mortals] and of angels, if we are not truly worshiping the living God, we are noisy gongs and clanging cymbals. Though we organize the liturgy most beautifully, if it does not enable us to worship the living God, we are mere ballet-dancers. Though we repave the floor and reface the stonework, though we balance our budgets and attract all the tourists, if we are not worshipping God, we are nothing.
>
> Worship is humble and glad; worship forgets itself in remembering God; worship celebrates the truth as God's truth, not its own. True worship doesn't put on a show or make a fuss; true worship isn't forced, isn't half-hearted, doesn't keep looking at its watch, doesn't worry what the person in the next pew may be doing. True worship is open to God, adoring God, waiting for God, trusting God even in the dark.
>
> Worship will never end; whether there be buildings, they will crumble; whether there be committees, they will fall asleep; whether there be budgets, they will add up to nothing. For we build for the present age, we discuss for the present age, and we pay for the present age; but when the age to come is here, the present age will be done away. For now we see the beauty of God

through a glass, darkly, but then face to face; now we appreciate only part, but then we shall affirm and appreciate God, even as the living God has affirmed and appreciated us. So now our tasks are worship, mission and management, these three; but the greatest of these is worship (Wright, pp. 8-9).

So what I'm writing is a kind of invitation to recognize the worth of God as you, again and again, enter into the grace of our Lord Jesus Christ, the love of God, and the communion of the Holy Spirit to worship.

For reflection and discussion

1. How do we keep God central to our worship?
2. It has been said that God is both subject and object of our worship. As subject, God is the one we are talking and singing *about*. As object, our praying and singing is directed *to* God. In what ways is God the subject of our worship? In what ways the object?
3. How have you experienced the presence of God in worship?

The problem of minimalism

I don't particularly like that word *minimalism*, but it's the only one I can think of to describe my concern, so please bear with it (and me). The case can be made that for centuries Western theology (developed by Roman Catholicism and its Protestant descendants) has assumed that the surest path to God is through the reasoning power of the human intellect. (The Eastern churches—those identified with the Orthodox tradition—are better at avoiding this kind of intellectualism.) According to the predominant Western way of thinking, God is, above all, a mind—a supremely gifted intelligence, overwhelming in its breadth and depth, razor-sharp in its power to discern true from false, virtue from vice. In short, we have been conditioned to believe that God is a cosmic intellect and that human intellects (however feeble and frail they may be) are the best examples of God's image in us. I remember in confirmation classes being taught that "the image of God" means we can reason; now I think "the image of God" means we can enter into relationships—but that's for another book. This intellectualism, this understanding of "God as mind" has been the fundamental tenor of Western theology.

In a number of ways, this understanding contributes remarkably to the sorry state of liturgical practice in many places. It fosters the minimalism that defines worship in terms of what can "get the job done," what is required but not what is necessarily at the heart of this enterprise. It helps make our churches look more like lecture halls than homes. It leads to sermons that are lectures on the geography of Palestine. It allows tasteless bread and cheap wine. It creates bizarre liturgical practice that says that a few drops of water from the tip of a rosebud connected perfunctorily to the Triune Name (and even that *Name* has sometimes been abandoned) is baptism in all its richness, which sounds more like dry cleaning than a washing. At the end of a service one Sunday morning at which baptism was celebrated in its fullness (thus making the service take longer than the requisite hour-at-the-most) a member said to me, "Gosh, that was long." My less-than-kind reply was a sarcastic, "Yeah, you'd think something really important happened, like dying and rising. . . ."

Minimalism can be traced through the Enlightenment and Rationalism, which led to American Revivalism, a trend still felt in our congregations. In the midst of this minimalism, American Lutherans have been "playing it safe" (for the most part) and keeping to ourselves. I think church historians are waiting for us to move from life at the fringe, from what Garrison Keillor correctly identifies as "shyness."

Most times I like that idea, our becoming more public. Sometimes it makes me tremble, and for some historical reasons. In the mid-nineteenth century people like Samuel S. Schmucker flirted with a phenomenon he called "American Lutheranism"—but the movement was quickly subverted by the huge new immigrations of the nineteenth century, by orthodox Lutheran theology and practice and by Lutheran separation, all of which were given the significant support of whole new populations of non-English-speaking Germans and Scandinavians. And so the question Schmucker raised, the question of how to be both Lutheran and American, was never actually engaged, only postponed.

I think it's being engaged now. And as I said, for the most part it's good we're engaging it. But we should take care. The Church Growth movement with its emphasis on personal decisions for Jesus, a virtually nonexistent sacramental theology, and a kind of entertainment that is neither worship nor evangelism has infiltrated many of our congregations. It has led to environments for worship in which there's not a cross in sight, the most prominent appointments being microphones, screens, and clocks (meant to guarantee that we not spend too much time worshiping God). It has led to theologically empty, musically soloistic, and, in fact, anticongregational songs.

No boats are coming now, so we panic. And the temptation is to look to American evangelicalism for un-Lutheran and, for that matter, un-catholic-with-a-small-c answers.

This approach is a great mistake. The secular press and even some of our Lutheran leaders have shown us in lurid detail the way in which evangelicals have continued the long American tradition of selling God. And we Lutherans have been captivated, tempted to follow suit.

It's interesting to note how some evangelical churches themselves are trying to recover their own sacramental roots; for some reason, that kind of information does not make it to us. An example from American history can bear this search out. The great Cane Ridge Assembly of August 1801, the beginning of what is called "The Second Great Awakening" was a sacrament meeting for baptism and for the Lord's supper on the Kentucky frontier. Though these sacraments were "upstaged" by manifestations of the Spirit, many evangelical churches know of that part of their history. Today they are moving toward more frequent celebrations of the Lord's supper, toward baptismal instruction (known traditionally as *catechesis*), and toward forming the assembly into a fuller expression as the people of God. So if we are flirting with evangelicalism, we should at least get the whole story and ask why evangelical communities are moving toward more sacramental practice.

Even as we ought to enter into fuller, stronger conversations with our evangelical sisters and brothers, we ought also remember that we have other sources for our life of worship. The question for us as Lutherans is whether our strong confessional devotion to assemblies gathered around word and sacrament—a devotion that is a presupposition of the Renewing Worship resources and the forms already in use in most of our congregations—can continue to find expression among us. Our remarkable vocation as Lutherans is to set into the mainstream of American religious and secular life a sacramental, gospel-centered witness to the triune God, enacted in open, participatory assemblies. Such a witness, such a sacramental evangelism, hardly exists in the United States today. We ought to get on with our task, the vocation God has given us.

The point of minimalism then is that Western theology says that the minimum *gives us enough to get by.* And I guess that's right: it *is* enough if all you are interested in is getting folks to join your club. But it's far from leading people to a fulsome relationship with God. Let me state it another way: Lutherans have used the word *adiaphora* to refer to things, especially in worship, that are "not necessary," things that are "optional." Vestments would be an example, or particular styles of music: things that are not essential to our worship. But at times we have "adiaphorized" the life right out of worship. We have identified as *adiaphora* so much of what is at the heart of our worship that we have pared down our practice to the point of being merely sufficient. It's as if we know what we *have* to do but we have lost the glory, the beauty, the power of what we *get* to do.

For reflection and discussion

1. What are signs of minimalism in your congregation's worship life?
2. What are signs of sacramental evangelism in your congregation's worship life?
3. What can we learn from other Christian communities? What can we teach them?
4. How should we determine what really matters, what is really central to our worship?
5. How can we make our worship more than just enough?

Signs and symbols

When I think about worship—when I think about God—I think in terms of signs and symbols. In a way, when we're thinking about God that's all we have to work with; even Moses wasn't allowed a face-to-face encounter. It's a problem, though. The church is not very good at identifying what signs and symbols *are* or how they *work*, partly because we think "the symbolic" is opposed to "the real" (there's that Western theological tradition again). Symbols and signs all too often are regarded as objects, pictures, or things that represent something else and thus have no independent life of their own.

I want to suggest that signs and symbols are neither objects nor are they representational, but, especially within the worshiping community, they are actions, they are verbs that create tension, clash, and movement. Think, for example, of a symbol or sign from language: a metaphor. A metaphor generates tension and clash by putting two things together that apparently don't belong together. Someone has said that encountering a good metaphor is like accidentally sitting on a porcupine: the event generates movement; if it doesn't, there's something wrong with you or the porcupine. Metaphor thus creates movement in language.

Christians have traditionally believed that the human encounter with God occurs within the media of signs and symbols and that those media are active, fleshly, historical, worldly. We are "incarnational" in our theology: Jesus' flesh and history are taken seriously. In fact, Jesus can be understood as a sign or a symbol of the transaction between God and humanity precisely because of his humanity, not in spite of it. Thus, Christians have classically resisted any doctrine that denies the true humanity of Jesus, because Jesus reveals God in our world precisely in and through the "transactions" of human flesh and blood. Jesus is the ultimate human being who lives, works, eats, drinks, listens, heals, talks, loves, blesses, and dies.

And what is true of Jesus as the ultimate sign or symbol is true of all signs and symbols: they work simply by being themselves. If one has to *make* a symbol mean something, then what one has is a mistake, not a symbol. If one has to explain the meaning of the appliquéd bird on a parament then the symbol is not working. If one has to label the candles on the Advent wreath or if they do not mark time because they are oil lamps, then the wreath is rather pointless. If one needs program notes to describe the anthem or the prelude, then the sign is not effective. Christian spirituality appeals to the ambiguous power of symbol and we who worship rely on that to a preeminent degree.

For reflection and discussion

1. This chapter gave a few examples of symbols or signs that I claim don't work very well. Can you think of signs or symbols in your worship space or service that *do* work well? Why is that so?
2. Would it help to think of worship as more related to poetry than prose? If so, how?
3. What in your experience (at worship or at other events) makes use of good signs or symbols?

3
It's *All* About Mission

Several years ago worship professors at the seminaries of the Evangelical Lutheran Church in America collaborated on a book entitled *Inside Out: Worship in an Age of Mission* (Fortress Press, 1999). This book speaks directly to two pressing concerns: worship and mission. All too often we think that worship and mission are "enemies," which is not the case.

A survey of congregations of the Evangelical Lutheran Church in America whose worship was regarded as "exemplary" by other people and who had sustained growth in worship attendance and membership reveals some interesting common characteristics between worship and mission. Here, in order, are the top ten, all of which were rated as "very important" by more than two-thirds of the people:

1. The preacher is a good public speaker, interesting and understandable, keeping my attention.
2. The sermon/message is based on the Bible and makes the Bible more clear to me.
3. The sermon/message helps me think about real life situations and apply faith to daily living.

4. Overall, when I worship here, I feel like I have been lifted out of my everyday world and been encountered by that which is holy.
5. Visitors and newcomers feel welcome and are able to participate in worship.
6. The prayers that we offer are prepared with care and include a wide range of meaningful concerns.
7. Children are welcome and generally feel comfortable in our worship.
8. Our worship folder or bulletin (and other helps) make the service easy to follow and participate in.
9. Music supports the congregation's worship and participation rather than being just a performance.
10. Our musical leader(s) are skilled. Their playing and singing show artistry and careful rehearsal.

These characteristics are central to our worship. So it might be interesting to have your congregation "rate" its worship. At a minimum, I think it would be helpful to talk about these things among yourselves in a conversation that invites the Holy Spirit to work at renewing worship in your congregation.

For reflection and discussion

1. Take another look at the top ten list. Are they characteristics of your assembly at worship?
2. Which ones are working well for your congregation? Which ones could use some improvement? What can you do to help?

Mission to a postmodern society

My second-favorite Christian musical group is Lost and Found. (They were my favorite until my son started another one.) One of the songs of these theologians, George Baum and Michael Bridges, entitled "Opener," is a longing plea that we "who have ears to hear" do hear in our world and in our congregations:

> I went to church on Sunday, just to hear good news
> and I confess it's been years more or less
> since I've warmed these pews.
> I am looking for something stronger
> than my own life these days,
> but the church of my childhood seems like the YMCA.
> . . .
> We just sing the songs we like to sing
> and we preach about the news
> and think up some new thing just to fill up the pews.
>
> I want palms on Palm Sunday, I want Pentecost still to be red.
> I want to drink of the wine and eat of the bread.
> But they strive for attendance while I starve for transcendence,
> But I count among this body both the living and the dead.

I want to focus on how the church ministers to people in postmodern times who are starving for transcendence. Does worship matter in our postmodern society?

First, a word about the term *postmodernism*, a term used in a wide variety of ways and covering a wide variety of ideas. In university history departments, postmodernism can lead to revisionist accounts of events, a prime example of which is the amazingly successful book, *The Da Vinci Code*—an interesting read and a masterpiece of revisionist history. One result of this kind of revisionism is an ever-increasing fracturing of society into various victim groups who are urged to tell their stories. People who accept postmodern theories claim that texts or paintings or music hold basically no meaning except what the individual reader or viewer or listener brings to them. But my concern is for how postmodern notions influence the people in our pews—or the people who are absent from them.

I guess postmodernism was inevitable because we believed so blindly and so firmly in the faulty Enlightenment notion of progress. With the rise of technology and science and economics and communications, the modern spirit insisted that "every day in every way we were getting better and better"—that we could solve the problems of the world with enough scientific discovery and technological fixes. But look what really happened. Instead of real progress, the twentieth century gave us disastrous world wars and depressions, the horrors of Auschwitz and Hiroshima, contemporary "ethnic cleansing" and tribalism, economic chaos, massive global unemployment, empty entertainment that keeps dramatically escalating in violence and immorality, and the obvious loss of any moral consensus or commitment to the common good.

The failure of "progress" leads to postmodern spirals of despair and hopelessness. The poor outlook for jobs leaves young people without any reason to learn. Most important of all, the failure of the hyped-up promises of science and technology accentuates the loss of truth already inherent in modernist relativizing and in the rejection of authoritative structures or persons with moral authority.

Consequently, the major characteristic of the postmodern condition is the repudiation of any truth that claims to be truly true. "Christianity might be true for you, but it's not for me," our children *used to say* with modernist relativity. Now they are learning that *any* claim to truth is merely a means to hide an oppressive will to power. The result is the malaise of meaninglessness, the inability to trust anyone, and the loss of any reference point by which to construct one's life. To this meaningless postmodern mess worship has much to offer.

For reflection and discussion

1. Is this an overstatement or do you think we are living in rootless, truthless times?
2. What can the church offer to this kind of society?
3. How can our worship be true for postmodern people?

Culture's contemporary challenge

The foregoing leads me to a question that looks at the tension between two approaches to culture: normative and empirical. A normative approach to culture views standards as universal, stable, and objective. So, for example, church musicians experience this by emphasizing one particular musical repertory as the most appropriate for all assemblies. The Second Vatican Council leaned this way when it declared that, all things being equal, Gregorian chant should be given "pride of place" in liturgical celebrations. (Much official and unofficial material in Lutheran circles these days seems to say that pop-rock is given pride of place.)

An empirical approach to culture sees standards as ever-changing and collective. This understanding suggests that beauty itself is directly related to the webs of significance that connect people; that is, values of beauty and form are clearly culturally influenced and may change from one generation to another.

The social diversity of the United States today is profound. In the past fifty years we have had few common experiences that bind together our geographical, educational, financial, or ethnic differences. Consequently, our society is fragmented into communities with unique viewpoints, experiences, goals, and traditions. Subgrouping seems to be more important in the formation of identity than does the collective whole.

Broad societal trends continue to affect the church's mission: personalism, localism, volunteerism, and individualism are among those that come to mind.

- *Personalism* leads people in society at large to make choices about their religious practice based not on birth or education but on individual preference. For those who long for strong education in a particular denomination's tradition, this trend is bad news. Because people are changing denominations at a rapidly increasing pace, realistic expectations for corporate memory are declining every day.

- *Localism* is another cultural trend in which the unofficial or the local is seen as being more trustworthy than the official, the national, or the international. For denominations that look for churchwide standards, uniform practices, ecclesially approved worship books, and anything approaching universality, this phenomenon is also bad news. The culture is quickly moving toward decentralization in which "make your own service, or hymnal, or creed" is an every-Sunday event.
- *Volunteerism* is another cultural leaning in which well-meaning volunteers are accepted as more knowledgeable than those who have profound experience and training. The church experiences this volunteerism clearly in its debates about theology, but perhaps even more profoundly in the area of worship leadership.
- *Individualism,* similar to but a bit more intense than personalism, is another trend. Even though more than 90 percent of people claim to believe in God, fewer than 40 percent participate in a congregation and even fewer in a worshiping assembly. Such corporate experience of worship, it seems, is not felt to be important.

In the face of these trends, the church needs to be far more intentional about renewing its worship on the basis of foundational practices of the faith. That is, patterns of faith and practice need to be infused with a renewed vigor and devotion.

For reflection and discussion
What signs of personalism, localism, volunteerism, and individualism do you see in your life and society? Are they helpful? Do they affect worship in your assembly?

Assembly required

What would a birthday party be like if no one sang "Happy Birthday"? What would a basketball game be like if no one cheered? What would Thanksgiving dinner be like if it was eaten in solitude or if those at table did not speak to one another? Now all of these events, all of these rituals, require special preparations and tasks: cake baking, cheerleading, sparking the conversation. But more than that, before all of that, these events need *people* who are to lend voices, hands, and hearts to make something happen, people who just want to be together and want to make that time a good time.

The various ministries of worship leadership are nothing without the assembly. It was not always so. (This is a bit of an overstatement, but bear with me.) When I was growing up we went to church and prayed and sang, but the pastor did all the work. (His wife was our organist and choir director, so it was really an in-house operation.) I vividly recall when our pastor began having acolytes light the candles. (Up until that time, he did that, too.) I would not be surprised if some of our congregation suggested a salary cut! But, when you think about it, remnants of that attitude still remain in our congregations. In a way, the good people who head straight for the back pews or try not to sit too close to anyone else or fold their arms across their chests at the greeting of peace are continuing that tradition. Worship for them has apparently become a spectator sport.

So let me be clear: all of the changes of the past thirty years are not for God's sake, they are for the sake of the assembly, they are to make us see our ministry and seize it. And if worship renewal seems not to have gone very far, it's because we've somehow forgotten the assembly. Presiding ministers, assisting ministers, readers, musicians, acolytes can only do so much; worship is done by the assembly and everything that the leaders do must have that assembly in mind. We need the assembly to shake each other's hands. But let's start at the beginning.

The first thing the assembly does is *assemble,* making one another welcome, taking places near the altar (*hint, hint*) and near one another. Assemblies have to gather together: that is as essential to the ministry of the assembly as a voice is to a singer. Worship does not happen in a bubble somewhere untouched by whether we smile at one another, whether we sit together, and whether we pay attention to each other. The liturgy is made possible and real (or turned into a lifeless abstraction) by such actions.

Another thing the assembly does is *listen*, which is its job at certain points, such as during the readings or sermon or the silences following them. In order to support its leaders, the assembly gives them its eyes, offers its full attention, reflects on what has been read, acclaims the gospel proclaimed, listens to the preacher, intercedes for the world and for the church.

The assembly also gives thanks. Acclamation is part of our job at worship, giving voice to our praise and thanksgiving. What would seem obvious perhaps isn't. We don't say "thank you" much any more; the cashier at Wal-Mart seems caught off-guard when I do. Our prayers even in corporate worship tend to be laundry lists of what we want from God. And we don't sing much in community. At the baseball game the singer gloriously improvises on the national anthem but the crowd is virtually silent. Being eucharistic—that is, being thankful—is a task the assembly needs to renew.

When I think about what a worshiping assembly should be and do, I look for participating people assembled around the word and the sacraments every Sunday, led by people who honor and serve the assembly and help it give voice to its praise and prayer. I look for the scriptures and the meal to be central in this gathering. I look for intercessory prayer on behalf of all God's people and all God's creation. I look for countercultural communal song. I look for this assembly to have an open door to all who would come and see—for all of its participants are seekers, all are beggars. I look for an assembly into which people are incorporated by the great and cleansing flood of Holy Baptism and in which baptismal signs and words are constantly present. I look for this assembly to connect with the daily life of its participants in profound ways that say that this assembly matters for the life of the world and not only for the needs of its members.

And here's the wonder that I rejoice in, here's the amazing truth I invite you to see and feel: we already *have* this assembly. We live in it. We work in it. Our assembly, whatever its ethnic origin or economic makeup, simply needs to be drawn again and again into these sources that will create and recreate it again and again. Our assembly, each time it gathers, craves renewing worship.

For reflection and discussion

1. What is your Sunday assembly like? Why do you attend? How does our motivation for "going to church" determine what we "get out of it"? Is it important to "get something out of" worship?
2. Are your assembly's leaders and participants fully engaged in their own ministries? Do readers and those who lead prayers prepare? Do assisting ministers realize that part of their leadership is to symbolize and represent all those gathered? Does the presiding minister let these ministries happen and in fact facilitate them by getting out of the way?

4
Defining Worship

We need to answer a basic question: What is worship? At times it is clear that not everyone knows. So let me try the following thoughts.

Worship is the language of adoration addressed to God *and* the language of God equipping us for life and witness. A friend of mine claims that the only person who has a "worship experience" is God, and there's truth in that clever turn of phrase, though it's not as *purely* true as my friend thinks! Good worship *will be* evangelistic, but evangelism is not its primary purpose, for worship is directed to God as its subject and object. Good worship will *both* nurture the character of believers and the community *and* form us to be the kind of people who will reach out in witness and service to the world.

Worship is ritual, not entertainment. In liturgical worship we use actions that are stylized and even exaggerated in order to draw the assembly together. In worship we use symbols that are common, yet take on different meaning in the context of the assembly. So our ritual speaks to us in ways that are not entertaining. Worship does not always have to be different, filled with new and exciting ways of doing things. It is meant to form us, not to have us on the edge of our seats.

Worship keeps bringing us back to the old words until we begin to know them by heart and to the old signs until we begin to see and feel what they mean. Our care should be to let the words be heard, to let the images shine, to let the gestures be done clearly so that they speak for themselves.

Worship offers a kind of order to the chaos of human life by providing a sense of stability for this assembly. This assembly raises the name of Christ in a society that is largely post-Christian. This assembly provides for outward-looking community in a culture characterized by, among other things, a rampant narcissism.

Worship affects the life of the world: the word and sacraments cast a new light on our situation, lessen or even remove the structures and systems that threaten human life, provide agendas for justice and equip people to follow those agendas, suggest meaning where before was only meaninglessness. So the liturgy is not only about God; it is also about our lives and our world in light of God. Our worship judges our lack of justice, our abuse of creation, our neglect of service to others, and it provokes us to new considerations of what it means to be the body of Christ in the world.

Worship is prayer. It involves prayerful togetherness, prayerful hearing of the word, prayerful concern for the world, prayerful acknowledgment of the gifts of God, and prayerful acceptance of God's commission to go and serve God in our lives. The place where the community gathers, wherever that may be, is not at that time a classroom or a dance hall or a theater or a cafeteria or a private chapel; it is a house of common prayer for the people of God.

Worship is not so much a celebration of life as we know it as it is a celebration of the life we hardly expect. Although it uses the stuff of everyday life—water, words, table, song, movement, meeting, touching, chairs, flowers—it uses them all with a sense of the holiness of these things, a holiness derived not so much from their presence in a sacred place as from a recognition of the sacred presence that pervades all places. The people and language and things of our worship are to be handled with reverence and care.

Worship is service. The German word for worship, *Gottesdienst* (literally "God's service"), is a wonderfully ambiguous term referring to our service of God, God's service of us, and the service we and God offer the world.

For reflection and discussion
What else is worship? What other words would you use to define it?

Truth-filled worship

Our worship needs the truth—the whole truth, nothing but the truth, so help us God—the truth that the church has to offer to people caught in what might be called "the postmodern condition." Let's begin by admitting what the scriptures teach: that our nature is helplessly sinful, hopelessly lost, a truth that forces us to see that we cannot know the truth entirely, that our eyes are blinded, that our understanding of God is only partial. But this reality does not negate the truth of God nor does it excuse us from sharing the truth with others.

Against the postmodern rejection of the possibility that any universal, overarching truth is true to all people in all places, Christianity can humbly suggest a nonoppressive, all-inclusive story of a triune God who creates, redeems, and unifies as manifestations of a perfect love for the whole world. We believe in a promising God who always keeps those promises—a truth clearly seen in the First Testament history of the Chosen People and in the history of Jesus of Nazareth, God's beloved Child, who died and rose again in fulfillment of God's promises. We believe that the truth of these scriptures will reach its ultimate fulfillment when Jesus comes again to bring God's promised gracious reign to fruition. Our faith assures us that God's reign already initiated gives us all that we most deeply need of hope, purpose, and fulfillment in this present life. And this truth is central to our worship. The God of eternal mystery has been revealed to us, a reality that invites us to worship. And so our worship needs to be structured as richly and deeply and *truly* as possible, so that we never lose sight of the fact that God is the one who calls us to come to worship and God is the one who receives our praise.

Our worship must contain nothing but the truth. Music, songs, readings, preaching, architecture, art, gesture, and environment are all means by which God invites, reveals, and forms us. For example, if we use shallow (and please note, I did not say simple—I said shallow) worship materials, they will not reveal the truth about God. Instead of revealing the truth about God, and about ourselves for that matter, they will shape shallow theology and form us superficially. Songs with cheap or sentimental lyrics or music belie the coherence and integrity of God.

But, lest I sound like I'm beating up on musicians, let me also say that sermons that draw attention to the preacher's clever eloquence, or are just a book review for the newest material from a self-help guru, or speak merely to the superficial wants of consumers, or offer lectures on word origins deprive the assembly of the formative power of the scriptural narratives. The scriptures proclaimed in the dialectics of law and gospel offer what we need: repentant insight, constant forgiveness, authentic security, unconditional love, absolute healing, fruitful freedom, compelling motivation, coherent guidance, and eternal hope.

Even though worship can never give us the whole truth all at once, it dare never give us untruth or less-than-truth. Our finite minds cannot begin to grasp all that there is to learn about God, but every time the assembly gathers we have the opportunity to add to our total store of truth. Only by God's grace and in the context of the Christian community can we share in worship services that present as much truth as possible. Against our postmodern rejection of the past and of authority we realize that we are greatly helped by the wisdom gathered throughout the church's existence, by history's sorting of the good from the less-than-good in hymns and rites and prayers and interpretations. Now it is our responsibility to sort through what is new in order to choose what is true: keeping God as the subject and object of our worship, nurturing the truthful character of individual believers, and forming the Christian community to be reaching out with the truth that we know.

The world that surrounds us yearns for stability, morality, security, transcendence, faith, hope, and love. These deep needs can only be met through the truth that comes from the One who meets our deepest needs.

For reflection and discussion

1. What hymns and prayers speak the truth to you?
2. What furnishings in your congregation's worship space speak of security, hope, guidance?
3. How does your assembly lay claim to the truth of the scriptures? Of preaching? Do you participate in the proclamation?

New "styles" in worship

For the sake of mission, outreach, evangelism, or a number of other words that are used interchangeably, our efforts have often focused on providing new styles, new idioms and, sometimes, new orders for worship. I'm increasingly convinced that this was an attempt to take the easy way (too easy) out of our dilemma. I'll try to explain my conviction.

In response to the downward trends in worship attendance that accompanied the massive changes in U.S. society since the 1960s—and it has been a gradual decline, not a sudden plunge—many congregations took drastic turns without adequate thinking about the implications for theology and for our congregations' lives. Let me share a few examples. In the face of our efforts at relativizing truth, some dispensed less truth instead of more, becoming therapeutic instead of theological. Some sacrificed content for form. Some confused worship with evangelism. Some confused evangelism with marketing. As society became more openly pluralistic and less supportive of Christianity in particular some congregations blurred their unique identity as the people of God rather than accentuating it with loving commitment. As the culture became more and more rootless, some denominations and individual congregations gave up their heritage as communities with long histories, deep roots, and global connections. In response to the increasing clamor for choice, some congregations fostered consumerism according to "felt needs" instead of embracing what is truly needed.

Please do not misunderstand. I am not advocating a wooden traditionalism. Jaroslav Pelikan wisely said that "tradition is the living faith of the dead; traditionalism is the dead faith of the living." And I think tradition is extremely important.

I believe we can escape the so-called "worship wars" by remembering that the church is a house filled with treasures old and new. As God's people beyond the limits of space and time, we are linked to all

God's people in the past *and* to all those yet to come. We need both continuity with our heritage and constant reformation.

The interest in mission, outreach, and evangelism remains important in reaching that great mass of humanity searching for transcendence. What is worrisome are the misconceptions that continue to thrive and an alarming lack of clarity as to what the evangel, the "good news," is. For example, people are still being told we should have at least two points of entry into our congregations—meaning at least two kinds of worship styles to attract seekers and keep the old-timers happy. This kind of thinking entails a few fatal flaws. First, those congregations that offer both contemporary and traditional services have not experienced significant numerical growth, so let's not be misled. Second, worship is not the point of entry, you are. And third, we are all seekers. (Recall Luther's famous deathbed remark: "We are all beggars.") The Bible does not say we are to worship God in order to attract unbelievers. We worship God because God is worth it; God is worthy of our praise.

On the other hand, and let me be equally clear about this point, the scriptures *do* say that we are all witnesses. Evangelism, mission, and outreach happen in our daily lives, in our regular encounters, in our simple conversations and our caring, and at evangelistic events that have a focus other than worship. We are called to bring people to worship God and we *can* do that. But evangelism is the *means* and worship is the end.

For reflection and discussion

1. How are mission and worship related in your assembly?
2. Does what you do invite people into relationship with God? Is your evangelical outreach designed to bring people to worship?
3. Do your service folders (a better term than *bulletin*, I think) give enough information but not too much?

User-friendly-ness

Another misconception frequently touted is that worship should be user-friendly. Of course, it should, as much as possible. In some worshiping assemblies, for example, the service folders are absolutely worthless. I am certainly not advocating worship that alienates or is totally inaccessible, but a word of caution is also in order. Being confronted by God is not always comfortable or comforting. God is not easily understandable, nor is it cozy to be a disciple. Annie Dillard paints this picture in *Teaching a Stone to Talk:*

> I have been attending Catholic Mass for only a year. Before that, the handiest church was Congregational. . . . Week after week I was moved by the pitiableness of the bare linoleum-floored sacristy [i.e., chancel] which no flowers could cheer or soften, by the terrible singing I so loved, by the fatigued Bible readings, the lagging emptiness and dilution of the liturgy, the horrifying vacuity of the sermon, and by the fog of dreary senselessness pervading the whole (Dillard, p. 27).

Dillard reports that the Roman Catholic church proved more innovative. On one occasion parishioners participated in the sacred supper accompanied by piano renditions from *The Sound of Music.* She continues:

> I would rather, I think, undergo the famous dark night of the soul than encounter in church the dread hootenanny. . . . A high school stage play is more polished than this service we have been rehearsing since the year one. In two thousand years, we have not worked out the kinks. We positively glorify them. Week after week we witness the same miracle: that God is so mighty he can stifle his own laughter. Week after week we witness the same miracle: that God, for reasons unfathomable, refrains from blowing our dancing bear act to smithereens (Dillard, pp. 20ff).

We must be careful not to offend other seekers, but we must also remember that Christ is a stone of stumbling and a rock of offense.

For reflection and discussion

Again ask: Does our assembly invite people to God? Can we be welcoming to one another—members and other seekers—and remember that worship is serious business?

Ecumenical consensus and Lutheran gifts

It's interesting to look back and realize how our families influence our lives. My mother was raised in the Reformed church tradition. My father was raised as a Roman Catholic. They compromised after a neighbor boldly said, "You ought to take those kids to church," and joined a Lutheran congregation in our small Midwest home town. They threw themselves into the life of the congregation. They became active leaders. We were at worship every Sunday, sitting toward the back, of course. I vividly recall my father bringing home the pastor's copy of *The Concordia Triglotta* so he could read the *Book of Concord* in which are contained the Confessions that define Lutheran belief. I also recall my paternal grandfather's funeral Mass at which none of us communed. My best friend was raised in the Roman Catholic church, though now he's an active United Methodist. My first church job was as the summer organist in that same United Methodist Church. These ecumenical experiences shaped my ecumenical and liturgical life.

What makes our worship *Lutheran* worship? This question can stand for many other questions, such as, What makes worship among Lutherans both evangelical and catholic? What sets our assemblies apart from those of our ecumenical sisters and brothers? What are distinctive marks of Lutheran assemblies gathered around word and sacraments? The first answer to all of these questions is "Not much" and the second answer is "Quite a bit, actually."

An amazing ecumenical consensus in worship, a common core of characteristics, can be seen in recent worship books in a great variety of denominations. This consensus can be articulated as follows: This assembly of Christians uses gracious, life-giving signs and strong, clear words. *Saying and doing* the good news of Jesus Christ in word and sacraments within a group of God's people is the central reality of much of Christian worship today. Because we have no empirical way to capture and express the essence of God, we construct worship using images, metaphors, and anthropomorphisms to express the gracious acts of God in their myriad forms. Our words, symbols, and gestures are profound and beautiful and include many of those images the scriptures use to express the idea of God.

The words and actions that form our worship use the expertise of various disciplines and the contributions of various ethnicities with the church's history and tradition, and they unite these gifts in the community's offering to God.

The entire assembly is drawn into the event and is represented by many different leaders, lay and ordained. The people of God assembled in community in this place are of great importance, always to be respected and welcomed into the common prayer and praise, and never to be made to feel incompetent. The presiding minister acts as a guide, directing these people to do their ministry in worship (and in daily life). Musical leaders are dedicated to helping the people of God, not entertaining them. Assisting ministers carry out a representational as well as a functional ministry as they act on behalf of the people. The life of the assembly itself is a gift; in the breaking of the bread and the sharing of the cup, people move beyond friendship to *koinonia,* the unity that is at the essence of the church.

Related to this *koinonia* is the desire of the assembly at worship to express its corporate character as the body of Christ in spite and because of its great diversity, as well as its link with the church throughout the world and throughout the ages. Thus the communion is both *in* and *as* the body of Christ.

Newly published worship books use amazingly similar terminology to identify the four-fold shape of worship in many churches: the *Gathering* of the people of God, a central focus on the *Word* of God read from scripture and proclaimed in sermon or homily, the importance of table fellowship with Christ and with Christ's people in the *Meal,* and a *Sending* into the world for continued service. Within this basic shape, some differences between the churches emerge, yet a consensus is marked by a simplicity that emphasizes the flow of the order while following this shape.

In her classic book *Worship,* Evelyn Underhill writes perceptively about Lutheran understandings of worship, beginning with Martin Luther's liturgical work. Luther did not seek to be an innovator but rather worked to restore the balance of word and sacrament, moving from the medieval emphasis on the meal that led to the near exclusion of the word. Underhill rightly claims that for Lutherans the word *is* a sacrament, the "sensible garment" in which the presence of God is clothed. But in the generations after Luther, the rhythm of divine initiative and human response was lost because of an overemphasis on the restoration of this balance, which, in fact, moved to the opposite of the medieval extreme. Thus, Luther's desire, while coming closer to being a reality among us through changes in eucharistic piety over the past half-century, remains an unmet goal. The meal is now secondary to the preaching of the word; when Lutherans greet their pastor on the way out of worship with "good job, Pastor" they usually mean that the sermon was satisfactory. However, the frequency of celebration of the Holy Communion is increasing in Lutheran congregations and appreciation for this sacrament continues to grow.

Some of the distinctive marks identified by the Lutheran Confessions themselves are becoming more common in our congregational practice. According to the *Augsburg Confession,* worship *defines* the church; Article 7 declares that the church is "the assembly of all believers among whom the gospel is purely preached and the holy sacraments are administered according to the gospel" (*The Book of Concord*, p. 42). In Lutheran churches we see signs that a new, vigorous, robust style of celebration is taking shape as theological and confessional awareness increases and ritual action becomes less threatening. Controversies of "high" versus "low" church are fading, largely due to a renewed appreciation for the abundance of ways to understand the Lord's supper, especially as identified in the Lutheran Confessions.

Lutherans say that communion is a "means" of grace; the forgiveness of sins is given through this means because, as the *Smalcald Articles* (3:8:10) declare, "God does not want to deal with us human beings, except by means of his external Word and sacrament." This gift is offered to the faithful "every Lord's day and on other festivals" according to the *Apology of the Augsburg Confession* (24:1) and even more frequently to judge by the *Large Catechism*'s (5:24) declaration that the Lord's supper "is given as a daily food and sustenance so that our faith may be refreshed and strengthened."

Lutherans say that the Lord's supper is *both* sacrifice and remembrance. The Lutheran Confessions do not shy away from the word *sacrifice* in reference to the mass. (They don't shy away from the word *mass* either!) Much controversy among Lutherans still surrounds the use of the word *sacrifice* but the *Apology of the Augsburg Confession* (24:19) helps clarify the legitimate, even necessary, use of the term:

> Now there are two, and no more than two, basic kinds of sacrifice. One is the atoning sacrifice, that is, a work of satisfaction for guilt and punishment that reconciles God, conciliates the wrath of God, or merits the forgiveness of sins for others. The other kind is the eucharistic sacrifice. It does not merit the forgiveness of sins or reconciliation but is rendered by those who have already been reconciled as a way for us to give thanks or express gratitude for having received forgiveness of sins and other benefits.

Thus, the Confessions reject the thought of the sacrament as a sacrifice of propitiation, but clearly understand the eucharist as a sacrifice of praise.

The element of "remembrance" likewise is central to Lutheran thought about the Lord's supper. This remembrance, however, understands Christ's sacrifice as a *present* event, here and now, with us still. This remembrance is articulated by doing what Jesus did: giving thanks. Though Luther removed eucharistic prayers in his liturgical reforms, thereby hoping to rid the church of the emphasis on propitiatory sacrifice, the situation is different today. The eucharistic prayer is itself a remembrance of God's mighty acts in salvation history and especially in the paschal mystery of Christ crucified and risen. In congregations where the "consecration" is reduced to the narrative words of institution we are taking immense risks: the risk of losing the connection with Jesus's own act of institution—*blessing God*. We risk missing an opportunity to remember the wonder of God's interaction with God's people throughout the ages by ignoring the ancient practice of prayers of thanksgiving (*berakhat*). And we risk a return to a "magic moment" of consecration in which the words change the elements, a notion that seems distinctly un-Lutheran. According to the Lutheran Confessions, we rely solely on the promise of God that we are receiving the body and blood of Christ; thus, strictly speaking, for Lutherans there *is* no consecration or certainly no "magic moment."

For reflection and discussion

1. Worship in another church. What is the same? What is different?
2. Is worship in your assembly shaped by the ecumenical consensus? Is worship in your assembly distinctively Lutheran? What difference does it make?

Numbers and intention

One of my hopes as a bishop of the church is the revitalization of congregations, and I believe renewing worship is central to this revitalization. The November/December 2002 issue of the Alban Institute's monthly magazine, *Congregations,* makes the case for what writer Diana Butler Bass calls "intentional congregations." I would offer the possibility that we might call them confessional and contextual congregations (which sounds very Lutheran to my ears). I urge you to read this article at http://www.alban.org and ponder it in its fullness, but I will attempt to do justice to it to whet your appetites.

These days folks in leadership throughout the church know the story of what Dr. Bass names "St. What-a-Surprise, a particularly vital, healthy, and growing congregation." (I hear this kind of story all the time from folks in various churches who are trying to encourage us to do this or that, use this program, ditch this practice, etc.)

What encourages the growth at "St. What-a-Surprise"? Dr. Bass groups such congregations into four categories: The first three types are familiar to us, and the fourth is one staring us in our faces but apparently still mysterious (Bass, 2002).

The first, the evangelical style as described in Dean Kelley's 1972 book, *Why Conservative Churches Are Growing*, claims congregations need to "embrace evangelicalism." Second, the new paradigm style attempts to imitate Willow Creek Community Church in Barrington, Illinois, a megachurch that promotes a user-friendly atmosphere. Third, the diagnostic style, based on psychological therapy and the social sciences, works to fix the systemic problems of congregations, which I define as twelve-step groups. I'll get to the fourth style soon.

The track record and potential of each of these first three styles is clearly successful in terms of numerical growth. But Dr. Bass finds enough *exceptions* to question how universal they might actually be. For example, she points to enough vital, thriving congregations ("St. What-a-Surprises") that are theologically "liberal," which suggests that a switch to a more conservative theology is not required. Enough of these congregations feature "traditional" liturgies and worship spaces to indicate that not all churchgoers are after a symbolically neutral (e.g., without crosses and such) worship service. And, finally, Dr. Bass notes, the presence of thoughtful, theologically mature congregational leaders with a sense of identity and vision within *both* declining *and* thriving congregations confirms that vitality depends on more than organization and leadership.

Those who study mainline churches (among them, I fear, certain Lutherans) have tended to miss a fourth category, what Dr. Bass calls the "intentional congregation." Although I don't like that name—we use *intentional* all too much—I think these congregations bear the marks of Lutheranism, marks we dare not lose. Dr. Bass writes, "These congregations form no national movement and claim no single source of inspiration. They have no party, no platform, no seminary, no publication, and no organization. Each is a unique and inventive blend of local vision [what I would call context], denominational identity [what I would call confessional integrity], and Christian practice [what I would call liturgy, catechesis, serious devotion to the scriptures, striving for justice, etc.]. Such congregations exist. I know. Over the years I have been a member of a few of them." She continues,

> Intentional congregations are neither "conservative" nor "liberal." They are not seeker-oriented, but seekers are attracted by their spiritual practices. Like any other human community, they have their share of conflict and dysfunction. These churches resist labeling, serve no identifiable theological "party," and reject programmatic fixes. Here's how I define them: In these congregations, transmission of identity, tradition, and practice occurs not by birth, and thus, it is not assumed; rather, transmission occurs through choice and through reflective engagement, as a process both individual and communal. These

churches tend to be theologically moderate-to-liberal and are reinvigorating historic practices based upon ancient Christian tradition; they might also be called "neo-traditional" because they reach back so as to move forward. In these congregations, people choose to embrace or recreate practices drawn from the long Christian tradition—practices that bind them together and connect them with older patterns of living as meaningful ways to relate to a post-Christian society.

For reflection and discussion

1. What creates vitality in your assembly?
2. Does your congregation "fit" into one of these categories? Does it fit into all of them in one way or another? What difference does it make?
3. How does your context help shape your assembly's worship practice?
4. How does your confessional identity help shape your assembly's worship practice?

5
Community Revived and Individuals Respected

I have railed against American rugged individualism (and how it rails against community) so much that I hesitate to express this hope, but I will. I hope that in our worship we reach a balance that offers revived communities and respected individuals simultaneously. In the face of American rugged individualism, we need the reminder that worship is about something other than confirming us in our individual ways. Worship shapes a common life, a life with others. It places individuals in community, and the people I talk to often express a deep need for such community. Worship at its best also resists nationalistic impulses, ideological movements, and utopian programs that seek to shape human communities and command the allegiance of individuals. The kind of community to which the church is committed is not determined by territory, ideology, or fantasy. It is a place where each individual stands before God's judgment and mercy and where the well-being of the least dare not be ignored. As Thomas Schattauer writes in the helpful book *Inside Out: Worship in an Age of Mission,*

The communal character of the liturgical assembly is a critical aspect of the mission of God in contemporary circumstances. On the one hand, it critiques every notion of the autonomous individual and affirms the fundamentally social nature of human existence. On the other hand, it critiques every form of human community that disregards the dignity and well-being of the individual, including the structures and practices of churchly life itself. This critique takes place because the church, constituted in its liturgical assembly, is a distinctive community amid the plurality of communities, the one community that refers us ultimately to the fellowship that God establishes and promises to be the destiny of human existence (*Inside Out,* p. 16).

For reflection and discussion

1. Does your assembly foster community and respect individuals?
2. Does your assembly foster allegiance to God rather than to other forces? (This might be a good time to think and talk about whether it's appropriate to have American flags or other powerful nationalistic or ideological symbols in worship spaces.)
3. How can your assembly allow for personal participation while strengthening community?

Cared-for languages

Leading worship compels a care for the various languages of worship—verbal and visual and musical—and includes being attentive to how we speak of the God who is beyond gender and how we speak as the people of God who are radically inclusive.

Consider this example: our faithfulness to tradition and our caring for literary art, I believe, should cause us to dismiss poetic treasures, even those with what might be called sexist language, only with great and careful discernment. Some of the linguistic tampering that occurred in the production of *Lutheran Book of Worship* was perhaps a worthy effort but less than satisfying. Some of the most easily accessible contemporary worship songs are grossly sexist, as well.

We need also to be aware of the amazing impact of the visual in our culture. I would urge great and careful discernment in this arena as well, that our efforts not be cheesy or manipulative. Herds of golden calves await our worship. This concern needs to extend to our gestures, too. I am convinced that those who are to preside at the liturgy, for example, should learn from dancers and actors. Two most formative books in this area include Gabe Huck's still-relevant and helpful *Liturgy with Style and Grace,* the title of which succinctly states an abiding hope, and William Seth Adams's *Shaped by Images,* which encourages readers to think and visualize more clearly about presiding at worship.

For reflection and discussion

1. Think of your favorite hymn. Does its language praise the God who is beyond gender? Does it offer new images or metaphors for God? Does it speak of a people who are a new creation in which there is neither male nor female, servant nor free? Should your favorite hymn do these things?

2. Think of the last movie you saw. Is there grist for the sermon mill in it? How does media shape your faith and worship?
3. What are some of the golden calves you are tempted to revere?
4. How does the way the presiding minister leads your assembly help or hinder worship?

Bodies

Thinking about the gestures of worship leaders leads to the source of those gestures: bodies. We sometimes say it so quickly, leaving hardly any time to think: "I believe in . . . the resurrection of the body." What a remarkable statement that is! What a confession to claim! Unlike some religions, even unlike some Christian interpretations, we think that bodies are important enough to be raised from the dead.

I think this importance is also seen in our worship. It is more than words. Our bodies are involved. We stand, we sit, we bow, we kneel, we raise our hands, we process, we receive a piece of bread in our hands, we take hold of a cup of wine to drink. These postures are second nature to most of us; we're hardly aware of how our bodies are involved in worship. So the question "Why?" is a good one.

We stand to begin; to welcome the gospel and to listen to it carefully; to make intercession before God; to pray the great prayer of thanksgiving (the eucharistic prayer); to eat our Lord's body and drink his blood (in many assemblies, though not all and not all the time); to take leave of the assembly. Standing shows respect for the assembly, for the gospel, for God.

We sit for the readings and the sermon; as the gifts of bread and wine are prepared; when keeping silence is all we can or should do. Sitting helps us be attentive, helps us ponder.

We kneel, sometimes to beg for mercy or to plead for the Holy Spirit to come upon us or to show how truly sorry we are. Kneeling is the posture of a servant and of a person in need. We're both. (Note that the Council of Nicaea in A.D. 325 banned kneeling during the Easter season. The reasoning was that, as Jesus was raised from the dead, so also Christ's body now can be up-standing. It's an interesting thought.)

For reflection and discussion

1. Why do we use particular postures in worship?
2. Why do we bow as the processional cross is carried past our place? As certain words or the name of Jesus is said? As we walk in front of the altar? As the bread and wine are lifted before us? Or, why don't we?
3. Does sitting for the sermon make it feel like watching television? Do postures encourage a sense that it is to be entertaining?
4. When should we kneel? Where? Why?

Moving

All of our lives we are learning to move in different ways. When our children were very, very young, my wife Lois and I would watch for the movement of their eyes following our faces. We rejoiced when they could hold up their heads by themselves, turn over, scoot across the floor, crawl, raise themselves to stand, and finally walk into our waiting arms. Soon they were running, skipping, jumping, bike riding, swimming, borrowing the car. (And we longed for the days when they crawled!)

Moving is important.

Parades remind us that getting there is at least half the fun; public transportation and traffic jams make us doubt that, but it's still true. After an illness or an accident, we are anxious to get back on our feet, and if that's not possible, we're eager to learn to move on crutches or in wheelchairs.

Moving is important.

It may seem odd to think of worship as a set of movements. On the contrary, we've been well taught to sit there and move as little as possible. But, in fact, worship is a series of ordered movements—a dance, in many ways.

Dozens (or, I hope, hundreds, thousands) of small processions, on foot, in cars or vans or buses bring us together to join our sisters and brothers in the worship that often begins with song and movement. We stand and sing, turn to face the cross carried in procession, clap our hands, sign ourselves in baptismal remembrance, pause for silence and prayer. We sit and raise our faces toward the people proclaiming God's word. We stand and participate in greeting the gospel. We bring our gifts of bread and wine and money to the table and we pray over them. We process to receive the body and blood of Jesus Christ. And we process again, back to our homes and work and world until the dance begins again when we next go to worship. It is a circle dance, one that ends to begin again, a dance made up of dozens of movements, small and large—bows, signs of the cross, hands lifted up or snapped together in praise or held out to receive bread and wine, gestures of greeting.

We learn these movements as we learned to crawl and walk and ride a bike, not for the sake of learning them but to bring us somewhere: home to God.

_____

For reflection and discussion

1. Imagine your congregation's worship done in mime—in complete silence, with no props. What motions does everyone do? Are these movements done deliberately, broadly and elegantly, or are they done hastily and haphazardly?
2. What do our movements say?

For the life of the world

I recently purchased and read (twice!) an amazing book on the basis of the catalog's blurb about it and its captivating title: *A Banqueter's Guide to the All-Night Soup Kitchen of the Kingdom of God*. It was written by Patrick T. McCormick, professor of Christian ethics at Gonzaga University, and as the title suggests, it is a richly laden table of insights following in the tradition of such thinkers as Virgil Michel, Dorothy Day, and Monika Hellwig. The book's central theme is the often ignored connection between worship and justice, the connection between re-membering ourselves to Christ and re-membering ourselves to the poor, the oppressed, the marginalized, the executed, the forgotten.

> . . . the Eucharist is a feast of remembrance, an *anamnesis* that opens us up to the dangerous memories of a Christ who stands with, embraces, and becomes one of the poor—who takes on the mortal and frail flesh of the hungry, sick, naked, homeless, dispossessed, and disappeared. In the Eucharist we are called to remember all the blessings we have received from God and all the ways in which neighbors, strangers, even enemies—indeed all other creatures—are part of this blessing. We are also called to remember all the ties and duties that bind us to others. Injustice begins with forgetting, with forgetting the faces and cries of the poor. In the Eucharist we are called to re-member ourselves to those we have forgotten, for we cannot remember Christ and forget the poor (McCormick, p. xi).

In this astonishing book McCormick uses four metaphors Christians have traditionally used to speak of worship: bread, table, body, and sacrifice. He explores them in such a way that our attention moves from our own participation to focus on the great mass of humanity whom Jesus instructed us to invite to our banquets, and reminds us that as Christ's living body we are to stand with and care for all the world's nobodies.

_____

For reflection and discussion

1. McCormick's quotation uses the poor as a sign of all in need. In what ways does worship in your assembly make you aware of the world? Of the poor? Of the great mass of humanity longing for bread or hope or relationship?
2. What is the relationship between being justified and doing justice?
3. What elements in worship point us specifically to the world?

6
A Form That Is Formative

A wise pastor once shared with me his three laws of liturgics: "If it's old, it's good; if it's in print, it's true; if they give you options, use them all." Although other writings in this series will delve into the *ordo* of worship, I do want to write a few things about worship in general that might begin to demonstrate how our worship forms can form us to the kind of vision Patrick McCormick suggests.

The preface to this volume included a reference to how my family worshiped when our children were small. From them I learned that children are formed as Christians through the experience of assembling faithfully. Our children knew the texts and tunes of the liturgy (and even some hymns) well before they were in kindergarten. They learned the sign of the cross by participating with their parents in that signing. They turned to face the procession because the assembly turned to face the procession. In some ways it's like patterning, a technique used by physical therapists to restore the use of limbs following disasters such as strokes. The therapists move the limbs for the victims until such a time as the victims are able to do so themselves. This form forms us, takes us from the font and shows us what baptism means, brings us to the table and feeds us what we need.

Another form or pattern that forms us in countercultural ways is the calendar. We gather for worship on Sundays while others are playing soccer or reading the newspaper. We hang on to Advent even though it starts way later than the Christmas shopping season. We teach that Easter is a season of Sundays and not just a single day. We let Lent renew us in our baptismal awareness and covenant. All these things, and more, form us as Christians so that we are able to be set apart, different, called out to witness to the world.

For reflection and discussion

1. What patterns are in your bones? What do you do by heart? How has worshiping with the assembly formed you as a Christian?
2. How does your assembly mark the seasons of the church's year? Are Sundays and seasons treated with integrity? What do we learn from such countercultural activities?

Gathering

Every day people gather at different times and in different groups at different places for different purposes. Sometimes the gathering is just to *be* there as a group of individuals together. We assemble at a bus stop, in the school auditorium, at the theater or the ball park. And just being there often is enough.

At other places we assemble to *do* something—to work, to have a party, to eat a meal. We talk to each other, we reach out our hand to each other, sometimes we even sing with each other. We participate in order to fulfill the purpose of that assembly, and if we don't then it's not an assembly but a group of people who happen to be in the same place at the same time. That's why our gathering for worship is significant in itself!

It's the church that gathers. More than that, the church gathers us for worship. If we waited until we were able to come to worship perfectly prepared, some of us would never get there. The reality for many of us is that we spend the time before arriving at church looking for a lost shoe, ironing the only clean blouse, arguing with offspring about why they have to go, or crawling behind a motorist driving ten miles under the speed limit.

Things are never the way they *should* be. But if we keep waiting for what *should* be we'll miss what is real!

We come to worship prepared as best we can be—accepting our imperfection. It is not an excuse; it's a fact. Luther, in his Small Catechism, reminds us that "a person who has faith in these words, 'given for you' and 'shed for you for the forgiveness of sins,' is really worthy and well prepared."

We leave behind a little of what distracts us. We greet one another. We sing together. We hear other voices, perfect and imperfect. We pray. We make the transition from the world of *should be* to the world of what is real, what really matters: the church assembled, warts and all, and Christ present in that assembly.

The first, most basic sign of God's redemptive intervention in human life is the existence of the assembly. Think about it. The reason we gather for worship is that God has called us together. It is our vocation. The assembly, lukewarm and listless, confused and prejudiced though it might be, is nevertheless the people of God, the sign set among the nations to testify to the reality of God and to God's concern for the human race. Of course, it might not be a very good sign of God's salvation. It can be riddled with cliques, smug and self-satisfied, lacking any sense of itself as a Christian community, rife with prejudice and soiled with injustice, its life shaped by the ways of the world and not by the ways of God. But it is still a sign of God's gracious love, the body of Christ in the world God loves. So the gathering is itself a sign of what God is doing and promises to do: to gather all people into one; to overcome divisions; to provide a place for the homeless and the lonely; to give support to those whose burdens are heavy; to create an oasis of community in the midst of a world painfully divided and individualized. This assembly is the anticipation of the day when God's reign will be established in all its fullness. Then there will be no more discrimination, no more hunger or thirst, no more mistrust and violence, no more competitiveness and abuse of power, for all things will be subject to Christ and God will reign over all in peace and forever.

> We assemble to praise and to thank God—together.
> We ask for God's blessing and we pray for all kinds of
>   people—together.
> We listen to the word and we sing—together.
> We receive Christ's own body and blood—together.

For reflection and discussion

1. What kind of an assembly are we when we gather for worship? Is just being there enough?

2. What does being the body of Christ mean? Where in this society that stresses individualism can we realize that together we are the body of Christ? If it's not when we come together for worship, then when is it? How does all this "togetherness" define us?

3. What is lost if we fail to welcome one another, sit close to one another, make it plain that it matters that we're worshiping together? In what ways can our congregation help bring people together instead of separating them?

4. Why is it important that worship involve all in the assembly? How does singing together, or making a gesture together, or saying "Amen" together help make us one people instead of roomful of individuals?

Word

The part of the service simply called Word is not instruction *about* God. It is the word *of* God addressed to us *by* God, which is different from religious instruction. Because some folks have not yet learned that difference, it cries out for care. The word is not talking *about* God; it is God speaking to us. God communicates not merely by putting thoughts into our heads or whispering in our ears, but by doing significant things in human lives. During this time we gather at the intersection of God's story and our story.

Alex Haley, the author of the book *Roots*, began the research of his family's heritage by recalling the stories his mother and grandmother told him as a child. Through research Haley was able to determine when and from what part of Africa his ancestor had been taken. Traveling there, Haley was invited to listen to the tribal history. At one point the elder told of Kunta Kinte, who had gone out from the village one day and never returned. And from the stories Haley heard as a child, he recognized it as the story of how his ancestor had been captured into slavery.

When we assemble for worship we hear *our* story. Our story begins with the Jewish people. Their tradition and ours is told in legends, parables, histories, genealogies, laws, customs, wise sayings, prophecy, letters, and songs. Whatever form they take, these scriptures tell the story of a God who made and loved a people, a God who chose a people who could reveal to all who God is because of their relationship with God.

The scriptures are the written memory of the people of God, the record of and reflection on the acts of God in the past. So what use is it to us? Why should we remember the past? Why do we keep on telling these old stories? We tell them because we recognize that these stories are *our* stories, that the people in them are our people, that the God who called and loved them calls and loves us and is fashioning us into a people who can reveal who God is to other people.

God still speaks in events and circumstances of our lives and times, but in order to interpret our lives in the present we must know what has happened in the past. The remembrance of the past is the key to understanding the present. We read the scriptures because they are the memory of God's people. They are not read simply for their own sakes, as people who keep rehearsing their memories and living in the past, but as the formative memory that makes the present intelligible, helping us understand our own lives and interpret the significant events in our world today as "word of God" events in which God is continuing to be active and present. That is why we read the scriptures and preach the scriptures.

A book can be a dangerous thing if people listen to it and live by it. To control people, the Nazis burned books they did not like. In the early church, too, a Roman soldier wrote of searching a Christian church and being disappointed at not finding the book (probably because some brave believer risked everything to hide it.)

Christians have always been people of the book, and for many that simply means the Bible. But in worship the book we hold central is the lectionary, that selection of specific readings for specific days. The lectionary is not a condensed version of the Bible but rather a set of particular scriptures for proclamation in the assembly. In fact, long before there was a written, published Bible, there were readings like this, small portions to be read aloud when the church gathered to do anything important. (For more background on the lectionary, see Gail Ramshaw's book in this series, *A Three-Year Banquet*.)

Our book is dangerous, though we may not know it. No Nazis or Romans are beating at the door to burn it, but if we listen carefully to what our book tells us, and if we try to live by it, we may very well get into trouble. Our book challenges the way of the world and the way of the church.

Perhaps we have grown too comfortable with our book. We treat it casually. We've heard the stories so many times that we barely listen to them any more. The words sound like so much blah-blah-blah. Our book asks hard questions like: Why does might have to make right? Why does money matter most? Or things? Why do people have to be hopeless or homeless? Our book tells amazing stories about God and about God's people and about us.

So, what can we do?

We can *listen*. We have to listen hard. We have to listen hard together. We have to pray that our readers and preachers do a good job. We have to expect that they will practice.

We can *ponder*. After a given reading or the sermon, we can provide substantial silence. Not "free time," not time to read the announcements, check your planner for the week (as a parishioner used to do), find the next hymn, or write the check for the collection. It is time to ponder—to ponder hard and to ponder together in a communion of quiet.

Maybe by listening and pondering we will begin to hear anew our dangerous book. Then we will risk everything by carrying its message into our world. Then strange and wonderful things will happen again. Then the Word will be made flesh again. This time, in our lives.

For reflection and discussion

1. In Hebrew, the word for word could also mean "gift," "event," "occasion." Is the word read and heard in our worship an "event" for you? What difference does it make? Push it a bit further: Has God stopped working? Has God no more to say? Are there no longer any significant events? Of course God still acts and still speaks, but how do we recognize God?

2. Is it possible to listen well when we are fiddling with inserts? Do we really need them? Do we really need pew Bibles? How do these things help or hinder our active listening?

3. How important are times of silence in your life? Can worship offer such times? And how long should these times of silence last? Should we even worry about how long they last?

4. It's interesting that on any Sunday we listen to more scriptures in many liturgical churches than in many so-called "Bible churches." In the course of three years, the lectionary provides the opportunity to hear much of the Bible. Is this hearing important? Why?

5. What can you do in your congregation to highlight the gifts that each biblical writer brings? For example, what is the difference between Matthew's story of Jesus and Mark's story of Jesus? What difference does it make?

Peace

"Peace," we say to others alongside us, in back, in front. "Peace," we say, and if you are my age perhaps you think of Woodstock, middle-class American kids costumed in cast-off clothing singing antiwar ballads, making signs similar to Churchill's V for victory. If you are older perhaps you think of Normandy and Tom Brokaw's "greatest generation." If you are *any* age you think of Iraq, Palestine, Afghanistan, your own city, your own family, your own life. In this world what does it mean for the assembly to say "Peace"?

Today, in our world and in our worship, we are reminded that the greeting of peace is a gift to an amazingly broad, plural "you." Decades of Victorian manners may suggest that "peace" is about my inner contentment, about patience and resignation, about subdued conversation rather than boisterous arguments. But the peace of Christ is something other than a preference for mellow personalities.

Peace comes in the assembly because Christ is in our midst. Peace is promised to all the disparate folks whom Christ has made into a new creation. Peace is the fullness of life the Hebrew scriptures promise. Peace is the road to freedom from slavery in Egypt and exile in Babylon. Peace is the risen life of Christ and of the Christian community.

This greeting is not merely sharing a nice hello with a friend, not only words of welcome to a stranger, not checking in on how Aunt Tillie is doing. It is the end of war. It is the reconciling of enemies. It is the rescue of the slaves. It is the resurrection of the dead. It is the demolition of barriers between us and God. It is the recreation of human life by the presence of the risen Christ.

For reflection and discussion

1. Does your assembly share this peace in its worship? Where does it happen in the order of service? Why does it happen there?
2. Does this greeting become a "liturgical scrimmage"? Is it a time for checking up on folks or for reconciliation or for something between those two?
3. Does it offer to people the peace of the risen Christ?

Meal

Here the four-fold pattern of Gathering, Word, Meal, Sending is met by another four-fold pattern. "Do this in remembrance of me." Do what? What did Jesus do that we are now to do in memory of him? What's the formative pattern? (Not "What Would Jesus Do?" but "What *Did* Jesus Do?")

From all accounts he was celebrating a meal, a ritual meal into which he inserted new meaning of his own so that it became a celebration of what God was accomplishing in Jesus. When he came to table with his disciples Jesus took bread, blessed God, broke the bread, and distributed it to them, saying "This is my body, given for you." And then he took a cup of wine. Again, he gave thanks to God, shared the cup with his disciples, and said, "Drink; this is the cup of my blood shed for you." So, here is a four-fold pattern *within* a four-fold pattern:

- The taking of the bread and the cup
- The thanksgiving to bless God
- The breaking of the bread
- The sharing of the bread and the cup

It is what Jesus did and told us to do in memory. And in this way, the memory of the Lord is preserved as something living and vital. This four-part pattern of the meal continues in the liturgy today when it is celebrated with respect for the integrity of the rite.

We need to restore some significance to that first action of giving gifts and preparing the table. For centuries, Christians brought bread and wine, wheat and oil and eggs and cheese and spare clothing—whatever they had—to the table. The offering was a time for redistributing the wealth of the community, so that no one grew fat while another starved, and no one kept coats in the closet while others shivered in the cold. They could not celebrate the memory of Jesus' gift of himself without themselves being generous with one another. Some bread and wine were selected from the gifts that had been brought and this select portion was placed on the table. The remainder of the gifts were taken out and distributed to the needy at the conclusion as the service continued in the world. I believe this also was part of the early Christians' response to Jesus' command, "Do this in remembrance of me." To remember Christ was not just to think about him: it was to live as he lived and to love as he loved. Remember, worship is marked by remembering the needs of the whole world.

Having taken these elements, Jesus said a blessing in keeping with Jewish prayer forms. Again, he did *not* bless the bread and wine in some sort of consecratory hocus-pocus; he blessed God the Father over the bread and wine, a prayer of praise recognizing the presence and action of God in all the events of life. The great thanksgiving, then, is the fulfillment of one part of Jesus' command to do this in memory of him; it is the blessing and praise of God the Father in memory of Jesus. If it is, are the simple words of institution doing what Jesus commanded?

The eucharistic prayer is thanksgiving for the heart of life as Christians understand it: for all of God's creation and especially for the saving work of Christ. It is proclaimed over bread and wine, symbols of what is most basic, food and drink from the tables of ordinary people. In this context, when we are focused on the foundations of our life, we also beg God for the abundance promised at this table to be shared with the whole world, with the church, with all who seek God, and with all who have gone before us.

The eucharistic prayer makes clear the character of the whole celebration as a celebration of Christ's death and resurrection. It is an act of remembering before God the sacrifice of Jesus who, in submission to his Father and for love of us all, did not try to evade death but let himself be crucified and killed. Remembering the death of Jesus is not something that can be done simply by thinking about it. Remembering Jesus dying and rising means living as he lived, thinking as he thought, acting as he acted. To remember the death of Jesus is not just to be moved to tears by old memories, but to heed the words of St. Paul: "Let the same mind be in you that was in Christ Jesus" (Phil. 2:5). There it is again: this is for the life of the world.

This prayer is the church's prayer, not the presiding minister's prayer. We all participate in it. We involve ourselves fully when we join our hearts to the words sung or spoken by the presiding minister, when we assume an attentive posture, when we raise our holy hands in prayer, when we put aside the book and listen, when we sing or speak our acclamations with full voice.

Ultimately, "eucharist"—thankfulness—is what our life as Christians is all about. Wherever we stand, in suffering or joy or confusion or routine, our life is always to be thanksgiving, always to be a sharing of God's abundance with all in need. The purpose of worship is not to give lip service to God, but to glorify God as Jesus glorified God. We glorify God by transforming our lives under the influence of the Spirit of God so that we become increasingly Christ-like in our devotion to God and to the welfare of others. Jesus glorified his Father before all by being totally given over to the Father's work in the world, no matter what the cost to himself. We celebrate the memory of Jesus by offering our own lives for the life of the world. So our worship is inseparable from our continuing conversion to a deeper life with God and to a more profound life of obedience and service.

For reflection and discussion

1. What does the bread look, smell, and taste like? Where does the wine come from and what color is it? Why is it important to know these things?

2. Why is the eucharistic prayer important? Does it sound and feel important as it is prayed in your congregation? Does it enable you to pray your own thanksgiving to God? Does it help you ascend into the mystery of God? Does it prepare you to stand among the company of heaven? Are you moved to lay down your life as Jesus did?

Communion with God and each other

We cry out a great "Amen" to conclude the eucharistic prayer. We move toward the table now. But first we pray the Lord's Prayer, the prayer all Christians share, the prayer that marks all kinds of moments.

Here, it is a sign of unity, words that we all can say or sing by heart. From here on it's clear that we are doing the assembly's work, not the presiding minister's. The words of the Lord's Prayer belong to us all. They sum up the basics of our life: praising God's holiness, praying for God's reign, asking for our daily bread.

From this prayer we move closer to communion. Our focus returns to the body of Christ broken for all, the blood of Christ poured out for all.

The breaking of the bread is of such importance in the history of liturgy that it is identified as one of the marks of the Christian community in the Book of Acts. It is basically a functional gesture: for a loaf to be shared among people it has to be broken. But the fact that only one loaf was to be divided among all those present struck Christians as being significant from the beginning. St. Paul put it well: "Because there is one bread, we who are many are one body, for we all partake of the one bread." The early Christians saw the eucharist as a sign of the new community God was establishing through the dying-rising Jesus and the outpouring of the Holy Spirit, a community that embraced man and woman, Jew and Gentile, slave and free, and ignored all the old historical enmities and all the accepted social and economic barriers between people.

The breaking of the bread holds a profound truth; it is a sign of the unity given us in Christ, a unity that triumphs over all human differences, prejudices, and inequalities. The breaking of bread is a sign of the irrelevance of our divisions and classes; in fact, the eucharist makes these divisions irrelevant. But we have to take that irrelevance seriously in our own lives, which means living as if there were no classes, no racial differences, no social or economic barriers between people. It means dropping our grudges and our suspicions and our prejudices. Put another way: Jesus did not leave us a sacramental theology; he left us the pattern of things to say and do and in this saying and doing we discover what he meant, we discover that we are called to share in the likeness of his dying and rising.

The fourth thing Jesus did was distribute the bread and wine to his disciples, telling them to eat and to drink. Often at the beginning of this time of communion we sing of the Lamb of God, praising Christ over and over for taking away our sins, asking again and again for mercy and for peace. We move to the table, singing again as another sign that we are one body. And here, in a morsel of bread and a sip of wine is a feast to satisfy our deepest hunger and thirst. *Our* deepest hunger and thirst—mine, yes, but my neighbor's too, and indeed the whole world's.

The Holy Communion is the sign of the common life we share in Christ, the sign of God's gracious love. So Saint Augustine comments that when the presiding minister says, "The body of Christ," and we say, "Amen," we are saying "Amen" to what we are, the body of Christ. What we are. Here worship and mission meet so strongly, so clearly, that we can hardly miss it. We are the body and blood of Christ. We are to live as Christ's body and blood in our homes, our schools, our workplaces, our neighborhoods, our world.

For reflection and discussion

1. How can we find ways of sharing this meal that help people realize they are communicating with one another in Christ rather than merely engaging in a me-and-Jesus blessing of American rugged individualism? What would it say for us to receive a piece from a single loaf

instead of a little individual wafer? What would it say for us to drink from a common cup?

2. What might we do with the communion procession that sets it apart from standing in line at Kmart (where I am always in the wrong lane)? How might we involve acolytes and processional torches in such a way that the communion procession *becomes* a procession?

3. In what ways could we encourage people to sing on the way to and from the communion, urging them to carry their books with them or using songs that are known by heart?

4. Can we do away with those mini-table blessings after each group of eight or twelve is done receiving? How do we bless each person and the body as a whole as we meet at table together?

Sending

And now we return to the larger pattern and the conclusion of the service as we are sent from this place into the world again. John F. Hoffmeyer, assistant professor of systematic theology at the Lutheran Theological Seminary at Philadelphia, wrote a stunning article entitled "The Missional Trinity" for the Summer 2001 issue of *dialog,* in which he focuses on the *Missio Dei*—the mission of God—in the life of the church. I want to quote it at some length because he speaks so eloquently of our call to go in peace:

> The question might well arise: Doesn't the church's liturgy encourage us to think of the church as "inside" and the world as "outside"? We gather for worship, are renewed by the Word in scripture, sermon, and sacrament, and then are sent in mission. Isn't our gathering a "coming out" of the world, even as the name *ek-klesia* denotes those who have been "called out"? Isn't the sending at the close of our liturgy precisely a sending "back into" the world, so that we can there carry out our mission as church? . . .
>
> The rhythmic movement of gathering in and being sent out is certainly embedded in our liturgy. But that rhythm has a complex structure that it must retain in order to be true to its source in the gospel. First, our gathering has a specific center. We gather around the crucified and risen Jesus Christ. Christ, though, is a very odd center. Christ is a center who is on the outside. One of the facts about Jesus that most consistently infuriated his seriously religious neighbors was that he insisted on hanging around with people on the "outside": tax collectors, various categories of women of low reputation, "sinners." As a victim of crucifixion, the most politically charged form of the death penalty in his time and place, Jesus was most decidedly on the outside: outside the city, outside the law, outside the bounds of public honor and respect. In the famous parable of the sheep

and the goats in Matthew 25, Jesus explicitly promises that he is to be found in those "on the outside" of society: the hungry, the sick, the imprisoned. Jesus' presence in the outside is invisible, so the "sheep" in the story don't even know that it is Jesus whom they are feeding, visiting, etc.

Likewise, our liturgy's "sending" is simultaneously a gathering. When we gather at the communion table we hear that we are participating in a "foretaste of the feast to come." We are anticipating the eschatological banquet in which all will have a place. This means, though, that in gathering apart as the church to eat the eucharistic meal, we threaten to contradict the very content of the meal as anticipation of the eschatological banquet. We threaten to become the church gathering to eat a meal separate from the rest of the world that "God so loved." We avert that threatened betrayal of the sense of the meal as long as our churchly eucharist functions as a symbol of the eschatological banquet. But our gathering at the Lord's table functions as such a symbol only as long as the gathering is open toward all the world. We enact that openness precisely as we go from our worship gatherings to share communion with the sick and homebound, to invite others to the next celebration of the eucharist, to fill grocery bags in food pantries, to advocate for legislation that will reduce the number of hungry people, to refuse to cross picket lines where workers are striking to be able to feed their families, etc. These actions, too, anticipate the day when all of us in God's world will sit down around God's table. These actions—the actions that we are "sent" to do as mission—are part of the Spirit's eschatological "in-gathering" for God's great banquet.

In these specific ways—and not by virtue of a vague affection for paradox—our gathering as church is a sending and our sending is a gathering. To neglect our missional sending as church is not just to be weak on mission while possibly still being strong on word and sacrament. To neglect our missional sending is to betray the inherent dynamic of word and sacrament (Hoffmeyer, pp. 109–110).

For reflection and discussion

What does our sending say about mission? Is it clear that we are moved forward into service in order to bear witness to God's creative and redeeming word in all the world? Does it focus on Christ, the center of our worship, who waits also outside our liturgy?

7
Shoulds and Shrubs

After reading through the preceding chapters, I'm reminded that one of the great dangers of writing about worship is that it might sound demanding, even legalistic. So I'd like to "soften the 'shoulds'" and celebrate what is happening as we gather.

In Mark 4:30-32, we read: "With what can we compare the kingdom of God, or what parable will we use for it? It is like a mustard seed, which, when sown upon the ground, is the smallest of all the seeds on earth; yet when it is sown it grows up and becomes *the greatest of all shrubs,* and puts forth large branches, so that the birds of the air can make nests in its shade" (emphasis mine).

My fondness for Mark's version of this parable, which also appears in Matthew's and Luke's accounts, arises because Matthew and Luke have the mustard seed grow into a great tree while Mark has it grow into a shrub. Part of its appeal is that it's a humorous parable about modest expectations. And because I'm determined to keep a sense of humor and maintain modest expectations, I am cautiously optimistic about the state of worship in the churches. I really do believe that we are growing, even if it's only into a shrub.

Most congregations seem to be moving forward, trying to figure out how to be faithful in the present situation. We use our various resources with varying degrees of insight.

Still, I'm optimistic as I see an increasing movement toward weekly eucharist.

Use of the Revised Common Lectionary is widespread, although not complete, and more often than not we are preaching on those readings.

Baptisms are in the presence of the whole congregation, even if the practice can hardly bear this sacrament's miraculous power and the rite is truncated for the sake of time.

Against the cultural expectations we *are* singing, sometimes vigorously, sometimes well.

For the most part, our congregations are not attempting to repristinate the worship of another age, are not staging a medieval pageant imagined by nineteenth-century Romantics, are not engaging in American consumerism.

The congregations of which I am aware, for the most part and to varying degrees of success, carry on, as they can, using the historic *ordo.*

So I'm not giving up. I'm going to keep my expectations modest. And I will continue to have a sense of humor even about these holy things and these holy people.

The goal is to avoid the hopelessness that will cave in to any of the circulating opinions and to continue to love the people while leading them into a deeper knowledge, awareness, and appropriation than they already have of worship matters. A favorite line from one of our eucharistic prayers reminds me that we worship "not as we ought but as we are able." This confession gives me hope and serves as a reminder of what really matters in worship matters.

No one ever said it had to be perfect. If we waited until we were able to worship perfectly, some of us would never worship. Our worship will never be adequate to the mystery it contains. More often than not, our celebrations will speak not only of the wonder of God but of the brokenness and limitations of those who celebrate. Too easily we become caught in a critical attitude and then become angry and frustrated with our sisters and brothers in Christ, even to the point where we can no longer give ourselves over to prayerful worship.

The only way out of that trap is to allow the Spirit of God to convert us, to transform our indignation into love. It does not mean giving up the efforts to improve our celebrations; it means recognizing that at the heart of our assembly stands Jesus Christ who emptied himself for our sakes, who had compassion on the multitude and fed them, who was treated as a fool and put to death by those who were exasperated by him. Worship is nothing more or less than love on its knees before the Beloved, God. Mission is love on its feet to serve God's beloved world. Together we know and feel God embracing us and thus being strengthened for service. And while I am optimistic, I also beg that our worship be centered on God in ritual, prayer, holy expectation and multilayered service; contain and convey the truth; form us in the image of Christ; and help us toward Christian maturity. I beg that our congregations be restored to communities that confess the faith in their own contexts, never forsaking the gospel of Jesus crucified and risen as we say and do that gospel. I beg that we care for our various languages about God and about ourselves. I beg that we not forsake the beauty of our inheritance. I beg that in the face of social patterns to the contrary, we commit ourselves to being communities in Christ, rejoicing in the company of each individual. I beg that we do justice. I beg that the vision of the Evangelical Lutheran Church in America's statement on the practice of word and sacraments, *The Use of the Means of Grace*, be lived in each assembly for the life of the world:

Baptism and baptismal catechesis join the baptized to the mission of Christ. Confession and absolution continually reconcile the baptized to the mission of Christ. Assembly itself, when that assembly is an open invitation to all people to gather around the truth and presence of Jesus Christ, is a witness to the world. The regular proclamation of Law and Gospel in scripture reading and preaching, tells the truth about life and death in all the world, calls us to faith in the life-giving God, and equips the believers for witness and service. Intercessory prayer makes mention of the needs of all the world and of all the church in mission. When a collection is received, it is intended for the support of mission and for the concrete needs of our neighbors who are sick, hurt, and hungry. The holy supper both feeds us with the body and blood of the Christ and awakens our care for the hungry ones of the earth. The dismissal from the service sends us in thanksgiving from what we have seen in God's holy gifts to service in God's beloved world (background 51A).

In the teaching and practice of congregations, the missional intention for the means of grace needs to be recalled. By God's gift, the Word and the Sacraments are set in the midst of the world, for the life of the world (background 51B).

The word *renewing* is a promise and a process, both noun and adjective. When put next to the core activity of the Christian assembly, *worship*, it offers a hope-filled invitation that

> What we call the beginning is often the end
> And to make an end is to make a beginning.
> The end is where we start from. . . .
> We shall not cease from exploration
> And the end of all our exploring
> Will be to arrive where we started
> And know the place for the first time.
> —T. S. Eliot, *Collected Poems 1909–1962*

Acknowledgments

Excerpts from the following sources are gratefully acknowledged:

Pages 10, 11, 84: "Little Gidding" in *Collected Poems 1909–1962* by T. S. Eliot. Copyright © 1963 Harcourt, Inc., © 1964, 1963 T. S. Eliot. Reprinted by permission of Harcourt, Inc. and Faber and Faber, Ltd.

Pages 14, 15-16: *For All God's Worth: True Worship and the Calling of the Church* by N. T. Wright. Copyright © 1997 Nicholas Thomas Wright. Reprinted by permission of the publishers William B. Eerdmans and SPCK.

Page 25: "Opener" by Lost And Found. Copyright © 1992 Lost And Found and Limb Records. www.speedwood.com. Used by permission.

Page 41: *Teaching a Stone to Talk: Expeditions and Encounters* by Annie Dillard. Copyright © 1982 Annie Dillard. Reprinted by permission of HarperCollins Publishers, Inc.

Pages 49-50: "A Tale of Two Churches" by Diana Butler Bass. Reprinted by permission from *Congregations*, Nov/Dec 2002 issue, © 2002. Published by the Alban Institute, Inc., 7315 Wisconsin Ave., Suite 1250W, Bethesda, MD 20814. All rights reserved.

Bibliography

Adams, William Seth. *Shaped by Images: One Who Presides.* St. Louis: Church Publishing, 1995.

Bass, Diana Butler. "A Tale of Two Churches." *Congregations,* November/December 2002 issue, © 2002. Published by the Alban Institute, Inc., Herndon, VA. All rights reserved. Available at http://www.alban.org. For an expanded version of this article, see *The Practicing Congregation: Imagining a New Old Church* by Diana Butler Bass, © 2004 the Alban Institute, Inc.

Baum, George, and Michael Bridges. "Opener" © 1992 LIMB Records/Lost And Found, Box 305, Lewiston, NY 14092.

Dillard, Annie. *Teaching a Stone to Talk.* New York: Harper Collins, 1982.

Eliot, T. S. *The Complete Poems and Plays, 1909–1950.* New York: Harcourt, Brace and Company, 1952.

Evangelical Lutheran Church in America. *The Use of the Means of Grace.* Fifth Biennial Churchwide Assembly of the ELCA, adopted August 19, 1997.

Hoffmeyer, John F. "The Missional Trinity." *dialog,* Summer 2001, pp. 108–111.

Huck, Gabe. *Liturgy with Style and Grace.* Chicago: Liturgy Training Publications, 1984.

Kolb, Robert, and Timothy J. Wengert, eds. *The Book of Concord: The Confessions of the Evangelical Lutheran Church.* Minneapolis: Fortress Press, 2000.

McCormick, Patrick T. *A Banqueter's Guide to the All-Night Soup Kitchen of the Kingdom of God.* Collegeville, MN: The Liturgical Press, 2004.

Ramshaw, Gail. *A Three-Year Banquet.* Minneapolis: Augsburg Fortress, 2004.

Schattauer, Thomas H., ed. *Inside Out: Worship in an Age of Mission.* Minneapolis: Fortress Press, 1999.

Wright, N. T. *For All God's Worth: True Worship and the Calling of the Church.* Grand Rapids: Eerdmans Publishing Co., 1997.

OTHER Worship Matters TITLES

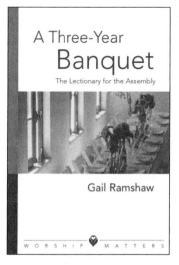

A Three-Year Banquet: The Lectionary for the Assembly
by Gail Ramshaw

A Three-Year Banquet invites the entire worshiping assembly, lay and clergy, to understand and delight in the three-year lectionary. The study guide explains how the Revised Common Lectionary was developed and how the gospels, the first readings, and the epistles are assigned. Further chapters describe many ways that the three readings affect the assembly's worship and the assembly itself. Like food at a banquet, the fare we enjoy in the lectionary nourishes us year after year.

0-8066-5105-9

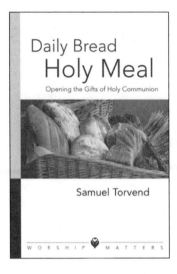

Daily Bread, Holy Meal: Opening the Gifts of Holy Communion
by Samuel Torvend

Daily Bread, Holy Meal invites Christians to reconsider the significance of eating and drinking with Jesus of Nazareth in a world of great need. Drawing on recent biblical and historical studies, this exploration of the Eucharist asks the seeker in every Christian to consider the ecological, theological, communal, and ethical dimensions of the Lord's supper. Through a careful weaving of biblical passages, medieval poetry, Luther's writings, familiar hymns, and newly-written liturgical texts, each chapter unfolds another "gift" of the Holy Communion and the sometimes troubling questions each one raises for individuals who live in a fast food culture yet seek community around a gracious table.

0-8066-5106-7

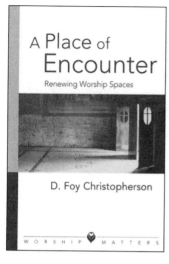

A Place of Encounter: Renewing Worship Spaces

by D. Foy Christopherson

House, temple, theatre, warehouse, courtroom, auditorium, TV studio, or lecture hall? River or baptistery or pool? Dining room or catacomb? House of God or house of the church? In its 2000-year history the church has tried on many buildings, and is ever seeking a more comfortable skin. Exactly what that skin will look like is guided by how the church understands itself, by how it worships, and by what it understands its mission to be. *A Place of Encounter* brings clarity and insight to congregations and individuals who are interested in exploring how our worship spaces serve, form, and proclaim.

0-8066-5107-5

CHECK OUT THESE
Lutheran Voices TITLES

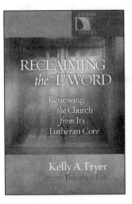

Reclaiming the "L" Word: Renewing the Church from Its Lutheran Core
by Kelly A. Fryer

Reclaiming the "L" Word is a book about renewing congregations by recognizing and living out the core teachings of the Lutheran faith. In the introduction, the author states:

> I hope that people of every denomination will find this book helpful as they wrestle with these important issues within their own traditions. But this little book is primarily written for those who call themselves Lutheran and, specifically, those who are members of ELCA congregations, and it is intended to help us answer central questions: Who are we? What *does* it mean to be a Lutheran today, anyway? And, why does it matter?"

Inspirational, engaging, and challenging, this book is a must-read for pastors and congregational leaders! **0-8066-4596-2**

Speaking of Trust: Conversing with Luther about the Sermon on the Mount
by Dr. Martin E. Marty

Speaking of Trust: Conversing with Luther about the Sermon on the Mount brings together passages from Luther's preaching on the Sermon on the Mount and Marty's comments about the place of trust in the life of faith. Marty has arranged Luther's words under three main topics: trust, prayer, and the Beatitudes. **0-8066-4994-1**

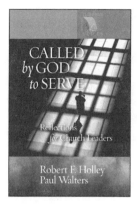

Called by God to Serve:
Reflections for Church Leaders
by The Rev. Robert F. Holley

Church councils and leadership groups will discover ten helpful devotional reflections and discussion starters for a three-year cycle, focusing on the task of serving from a biblical and theological perspective. Insights from family systems theory provide a framework for the reflections. Through discussion of theory and by encountering and responding to real-life situations, participants will ponder aspects of what they are called to do together. **0-8066-5172-5**

Leading on Purpose:
Intentionality and Teaming in Congregational Life
by Eric Burtness

Exploring the Purpose-Driven Church phenomenon, Eric Burtness provides pastors and church leaders with a Lutheran view of what it means to lead on purpose and integrates the Purpose-Driven philosophy into the context of Lutheran congregational life. He tells the stories of numerous Lutheran congregations, large and small, rural and urban, that have used this structure and ministry emphasis for health, growth, and revitalization.
0-8066-5174-1

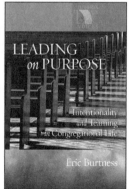

On a Wing and a Prayer: Faithful Leadership in the 21st Century
by Michael L. Cooper-White

On a Wing and a Prayer: Faithful Leadership in the 21st Century uses the language of aviation to look at the principles of leadership and apply them to congregations and other organizations. Concepts such as visioning, strategic planning, calculated risk-taking, flexibility, and discovering the gifts of others are included. The book also will encourage lay readers to consider how these principles can shape their daily lives and arenas where they live their Christian vocations. **0-8066-4992-5**

Our Lives Are Not Our Own: Saying "Yes" to God
by Harold Eppley and Rochelle Melander

Our Lives Are Not Our Own: Saying "Yes" to God is designed to encourage personal reflection and create dialogue about Christian accountability. God's gracious act of love for us in Jesus Christ affects not only our salvation but also the choices we make in our lives. God calls us to the blessing of accountability, not the burden. How do we say "yes" to God with our time, financial resources, physical needs, relationships, and in our care for the environment?

This readable and engaging book provides an even fuller articulation of the meaning behind the We Say Yes! stewardship program. As authors Melander and Eppley write, "God's saving act in Jesus does more than free us from the bondage of sin. God's act frees us for service to God, the community of faith, and the world. In loving gratitude to God for all that God has done for us, we live accountable both to God and to one another."
0-8066-4999-2

Who Do You Say That I Am? 21st Century Preaching
by Susan K. Hedahl

Who Do You Say That I Am? 21st Century Preaching provides some basic definitions of preaching in the post-modern age, a discussion of the basic theological gifts of Lutheranism, the importance of imagery in 21st century preaching, and the role preaching plays in evangelism in the post-modern age.
0-8066-4990-9

Signs of Belonging: Luther's Marks of the Church and the Christian Life
by Mary E. Hinkle

Signs of Belonging: Luther's Marks of the Church and the Christian Life explores Luther's teaching on the seven marks of the church: possession of the Word, Baptism, Sacrament of the Altar, Office of the Keys, Office of Ministry, Discipleship, and the cross (suffering on account of one's faith). How do these "marks" define the corporate body of Christ and connect with the lives of individual Christians? **0-8066-4997-6**

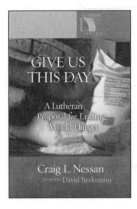

Give Us This Day:
A Lutheran Proposal
for Ending World Hunger
by Craig L. Nessan

Concern for the hungry belongs to the heart of the Scripture's testimony about God. The Bible's justice tradition serves as a canon within the canon that the Christian church dare not ignore. The Lord's Prayer demonstrates how justice for the hungry is also deeply rooted in the teaching of Jesus. The author summons the Christian church to listen to the cries of the hungry and commit itself to ending hunger as a matter of *status confessionis.* Ending hunger is a real possibility for our time. The role of the church in advocating this possibility is crucial. **0-8066-4993-3**

Open the Doors and See All the People:
Stories of Church Identity and Vocation
by Norma Cook Everist

Emerging from the author's interviews and interactions with numerous Lutheran congregations across the country, this book explores how congregations are determining and living out their identity. Their stories are intended to encourage and inspire other Lutheran congregations to take a close look at their own contexts and plan for the future. Questions and activities for reflection make this a great tool for congregational planning and development. **0-8066-5161-X**

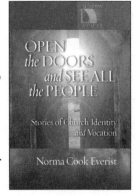